4TH FLOOR GALLERY

GUESTROOM TOWER

Hotel Murano: The Collection is unique in the world in that it concentrates on art made of glass in the 21st-century placed in a hotel setting for the enjoyment of guests and visitors. A blend of specially commissioned works and others acquired from artists' studios and galleries, the 45 artists from 12 countries on five continents (Asia, Australia, Europe, Latin and North America) are represented throughout public and private spaces in the building. Displayed within the hotel's indoor public areas and, in one case, outdoors, the vessels, sculptures, prints and drawings are joined by designed functional handmade objects and installations that assemble into a sparkling environment. Collectively, they provide an aesthetic envelope for the interested hotel guest and docent-guided visitors to learn about and enjoy the beauty of glass.

Curator Tessa Papas traveled the globe to find and put into motion the creations of glass that stud the hotel's newly refurbished and redesigned interior areas. The Collection fits into seven broad categories: major commissions; commissions for the hotel tower elevator lobbies; commissions that are a part of the hotel's design environment; objects and vessels that carry a symbolic or ceremonial character; abstract art; sculptures with animal imagery and those that use the human figure to tell a story.

Upon approaching the hotel, the guest and visitor are greeted by *Orizon* (2008), a monumental, 75-foot-high curved steel arc with sandwiched plate glass by prominent Greek artist Costas Varotsos. Resembling the prow of a ship, *Orizon* begins two of the most important themes within The Collection: travel and transportation.

Inside the lobby and suspended above the Grand Corridor, Danish artist Vibeke Skov displays three giant boats. The first, *The Boat of the Gods* (2007), deals with male myths of the Norse gods; *Creation*, the second, has images of the origins of the world; and *Goddesses* incorporates Adam and Eve, all of which employ fused, painted, slumped and cast-relief techniques.

The third-largest commission is Andrea Morucchio's *Laudes Regiae* (2006). "*Praise to the Crown*" is the Italian artist's homage to the Middle Ages. With a soundtrack activated for events held in The Gallery private dining room adjacent to the hotel's signature restaurant, Bite, *Laudes Regiae* contains 17 glass-helmeted heads on a wall, reminiscent of medieval banqueting halls and coronation decorations. The basic helmet is based on that of Attila the Hun on view in the Doges' Palace. An optional video projection is also periodically included and available for special events.

Creation (2007) by Venetian glassblowing virtuoso Lucio Bubacco refers to the creation of glass, not the world, to which Skov alludes in her *Viking Boats*. Instead, the elaborate work depicting eight male glassblowers and one woman technician is topped by a tongue-in-cheek homage to maestro Dale Chihuly with a conductor's baton, drawing attention to the complex teamwork required for glassmaking. Cupids accompanying the blowers are there for good luck.

Rick Beck (U.S.), Steffen Dam (Denmark), Deborah Sandersley (United Kingdom), April Surgent (U.S.) and Cappy Thompson (U.S.) are artists with other significant commissions in The Collection.

Beck's two amusing *Fish Lures* (2007) are giant glass castings that emphasize a favored Northwest leisure-time activity. Dam's *Specimen Block* (2007) encases glass versions of souvenirs from a nature trek: shells, maritime flora and fauna. Sandersley's *Biot Triptych* (2007) is a more explicit reference to travel. Blending and overlapping photo-etched memories of the South of France, three adjacent "shadow boxes" recall a dreamy villa; palm trees; iron gates; and two women in traditional Japanese attire, among other exotic images. As many artists in The Collection use photography and glass together, Sandersley's approach becomes timely and contemporary. So is Surgent's. Her two multi-panel photo-etched commissions, *I'll Watch the Road* and *By the Guidance of the Crow* (2007), treat the sites of rural electrification and wind-turbine power technology as worthy travel destinations as well as symbols of energy systems and the changing face of the Far West. Thompson's *Bee Deva* (2007) returns us to another medieval technique, painted glass, and the allegorical world of illuminated manuscripts. Two figures, one praying, the other hovering or flying, surround a beehive. Thompson's feathered, haloed goddess is another image of travel, the flight of the bee from flower to flower, fertilizing the garden and, in turn, making our world grow into something more beautiful and bountiful.

In the Tower housing guestrooms, seven artists received special commissions for areas adjacent to the elevators: Peter Bremers (Netherlands); Miriam di Fiore (Argentina/Italy); Tobias Møhl (Denmark); Masayo Odahashi (Japan); Peter Powning (Canada); Bertil Vallien (Sweden); and Toots Zynsky (U.S.). Within the group, Vallien is the most prominent. His cast-glass boat *Journey*

X (2007) contains glass inclusions resembling an eye, a starfish, a coin, a ladder, and other elements evocative of Sweden's illustrious history of maritime exploration, conquest and travel.

Bremers's *Iceberg* (2007) complements Vallien's Scandinavian approach to subject matter and technique: it is cold and cast. Born in Argentina, but long resident in Italy, di Fiore extends the travel theme in *Remember Me in January* (2007) with its photo-based rustic winter scene, perhaps an Italian river.

Møhl's *Nests* (2007) enhance di Fiore's mood of nature with his icy, clear and cloudy blown-glass objects.

Odahashi builds on Vallien's boat motif in her *Face to Face* (2007). Two women are at either end of a canoe; one is wearing a rabbit's-head costume headpiece. The precarious balance of the two in the boat symbolizes the necessity of humans working together to preserve and protect wildlife. Powning's *Essential Self* (2007) resembles 18th-century samurai armor using glass in place of leather, metal and fabric.

Zynsky's tour-de-force *Ventura* (2007) introduces fused glass threads (a technique she invented with Mathijs Teunissen van Manen in 1982). This allows for the fluid appearance of the vivid red, orange and black basket shape. All the experimental, loose-looking vessels in The Collection are indebted to Dale Chihuly whose *Macchia Series, Nested* (1984) is near the exact center of the wall display by the front desk.

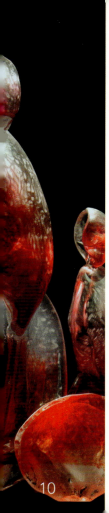

Glass has played an important role in the evolution of international design, something that Italian artists are particularly well equipped to handle. After Varotsos's huge *Orizon*, Massimo Micheluzzi's blown-and-silvered chandelier in the hotel lobby is the collection's second-largest commission. With its octopus-like tentacles and exterior rather than interior illumination, it contrasts nicely with the severe geometry of the building's architecture and interior design. Much more severe and colorful, the check-in area of the hotel's front desk is faced with an illuminated band of fused glass strips by Orfeo Quagliata, an Italian-born artist who resides in Mexico City. He also made glass door pulls for the hotel's main entry as well as the elevator interiors and sinks for the public restrooms. Varotsos's other commission is an entry-area glass mural, *Totem* (2008).

Elsewhere in public and private areas are two-dimensional works on paper by The Collection artists including etchings, prints and drawings by Dale Chihuly, Cobi Cockburn, Odahashi, Seth Randall, Bruno Romanelli, Bertil Vallien, and Janusz Walentynowicz. Eleven pastel and charcoal drawings by Martin Blank are another special commission. Most of these works are on view near the Mezzanine Corridor, meeting rooms, and boardrooms.

The earliest glass forms were containers. Besides Persian teardrop holders and Roman perfume flasks, Dale Chihuly's *Macchia* along with Dante Marioni's *Trio* (2006) offer bravura examples of the huge influence Venetian glassblowing has had on American glass art. Other artists turned the basic blown-vessel premise into a focus on stylized, imaginary functional objects. For example,

Davide Salvadore's *Spingarpa* (2007) exposes intricate carving techniques among a profusion of other elaborate approaches in his fantasia on Southeast Asian musical instruments. Setting up a Pop art contrast, Flo Perkins constructed the amusingly lopsided bowling ball pin, *Bowled Over* (2006). Brent Kee Young made two see-through rowboat oars, *Pull... Earl* (2006), using lampworking technique, carefully "welding" together tiny strands of Pyrex glass. Polish-born Walentynowicz made a contemporary container—a see-through purse holding a revolver—in *Purse* (2006).

It is eons away from the ceremonial mood of Pacific Northwest Native American culture in *Oyster Catcher Rattle* (2006) by Preston Singletary. With its two figures astride a raven-shaped boat, this work demonstrates the broad cultural applications of 21st-century glass.

Four works create a breathing space for abstraction, the dominant art style of the preceding 20th century. Steve Klein fashioned *Balance 52* (2006), a grooved black seesaw with green, orange, blue and purple balls.

Similarly, Australian-born Cobi Cockburn's *Shifting Seasons* (2006) balances another long piece, but one with two walls and a central pivot area. With its complicated linear surface pattern of "cold-carving" (actions undertaken after heating glass in a kiln and then cooling it), this work is less brilliantly colored than the Americans and Italians, something common to much recent Antipodean glass: cool, frosty or clear, and elegant.

Janice Vitkovsky, also of Australia, continues the new national style in *Moment When Darkness* (2007) with hundreds of tiny black murrine, or sliced glass caning, embedded in a pale pink and white background.

Maurizio Donelli's *Musicale* (2004) employs spirals and curves as colorful metaphors for sound and musical notes.

Animal imagery in the work of William Morris, Hiroshi Yamano and Richard Whiteley stresses another overarching theme within The Collection: ecology and the natural equipoise of the planet. Morris's *Idolito* (2004) is a horned deer or elk-like effigy awaiting imaginary idol worship. It borders on the ceremonial while Whiteley's *Blue Fin* (2001) echoes the pale colors of the other Australians and alludes to endangered species of the seven seas.

Yamano's silver and gold fish on his *Fish Hanger #49* (2005) honor a central food source and focus of admiration in Japan. They are an eternal motif in Japanese decorative arts.

The human figure dominates the remainder of The Collection. Ross Richmond and Bruno Romanelli isolate the human head in, respectively, *Ripple* (2003), a remarkably life-like cast-glass head, and *Sleep of Reason* (2004), whose title echoes the title of a famous Goya etching, *The Sleep of Reason Produces Monsters* (1810), that questions the cult of reason during the Enlightenment.

Seth Randall continues the references to older cultures in his *Akhenaton* (2002) executed in the unusual glass-paste, or pâte-de-verre, technique, probably invented by the Egyptians and honored here in a red, green and blue vessel with two opposing heads.

Alberto Gambale's *Tipo Veneziano (Venetian Guy*, 2001) is a whimsical gondolier flattened and abstracted with the characteristic horizontal-striped shirt. It joins a full-length Italian figure, *Dreamer #1* (2002) by Narcissus Quagliata. This wall-mounted work supplements other full-length figures by Catharine Newell and Karen LaMonte.

Newell's *Balancing Act IV* (2006) draws on photographed dance imagery with its reclining figures on a flat surface.

The centerpiece in the hotel lobby, LaMonte's *Pianist's Dress* (2005), omits body parts such as head and hands in favor of a massively detailed casting of the garment that recalls a triumphal Greek marble statue such as *Victory of Samothrace* (c. 200 B.C.) in the Louvre.

More humorous yet deriving from feminist art of the 1970s, Susan Taylor Glasgow's *Happily Ever After* (2006) explodes the myth of courtship in the form of an elaborately ornate yet confining bustier or torso corset.

Equally entertaining, *Homage to the Implant* (2006) by Jessica Townsend addresses women's body image in its installation of 18 blown-glass breasts. With great color and wit, she underscores the timeless place of the breast in art history.

Dealing with the overlay of women's memories in *Still Life I* (2000), Czech artist Dana Zameçnikova stacks see-through panels of blurred photographs, art-historical fragments, and personal mementoes. She demonstrates the evolution of European flat glass from stained-and-leaded to poured, tinted and laminated.

The final group, storytelling with the human figure, affirms the global nature of both glass and artistic culture today. Groups of male and female figures in the work of Martin Blank, Allison Kinnaird, Pat Owens and Therman Statom sum up the complexity and diversity embodied throughout The Collection.

Statom's 12 painted-glass playing-card deck characters include queen of hearts, jack of hearts, king of clubs, and the lucky ace of diamonds. They create a dramatic backdrop of leisure and chance, risk and playful uncertainty, for the Bite restaurant.

Enclosed in a niche near the Grand Corridor, Alison Kinnaird's *Interface* (2007) uses engraving to illustrate male and female nude couples in profile and frontal poses that emerge from dance choreography and martial arts. In vivid shades of red and blue, *Interface* is one of two culminating works in The Collection that stress social rituals.

Appropriately reflecting the myriad activities within a hotel, *Interface* joins all the other artworks on view in celebrating social events along with creativity, technical excellence, nature, and global travel as symbolized by the many ways glass art conveys a multitude of differing world views and legends.

MATTHEW KANGAS, prominent art critic, is the author of several collections of his writings, including *Return to the Viewer: Selected Art Reviews* (Midmarch Arts Press). He lives in Seattle.

PHOTO © CHRISTOPHER DAHL

Orizon
steel, stacked plate glass, 2008

"As an artist, I do not simply place a foreign object in a setting. Rather, I seek to reveal the idiosyncrasies of a site and its surroundings in a style that the public at large can appreciate."

After four days of studying the hotel site in November 2006 Costas drew a design for a sculpture on a table napkin. That design is now a minimalistic, almost two dimensional, 100-foot tall sculpture that stands outside the Hotel Murano today. Andrea Bellini, art historian, critic and curator says of Costas' work, "In general, even when his sculptures reflect a more complex and arduous structural approach, they assume a quality of lightness and immateriality which renders them almost virtual, image-like; a mental projection."*

*From Bellini's essay in Varotsos published by Futura, "Costas Varotsos: Along an ideal line between tradition and renewal."

Costas Varotsos, born 1955 in Athens, Greece, lives and works on the island of Aegina, Greece.

Front desk
fused glass, 2007
Door Pulls
fused glass, 2007
Elevator cabs
fused glass, 2008
Public restrooms wash basins
fused glass, 2007

"My most recent Geometry Series is composed of bands of fused glass in which I often trap color or light between layered sheets. Cutting away interior sections to reveal images between the walls of opacity, I then create a microclimate contained between layers. Metaphorically, it is the creation of a separate world between the lines. I use these solid elements to make the observer ask why, and search for the reward that is often not directly on the surface, but hidden between the layers."

Orfeo Quagliata, born 1972 in San Francisco, CA, lives and works in Mexico City, Mexico.

Dreamer #1
kilnformed glass, 2002

"We are alive in a very unusual state of continuous change. We are even a mystery to ourselves, not to speak of others. …. To me, this medium of glass is the perfect material to articulate how the essential soul, light, merges with the corporeal body, the glass."

Three areas are the focus of Quagliata's artistic activity:
- The exploration of light and glass as vehicles of artistic expression.
- A lifelong fascination with the figure.
- An active interest in how art can impact our lives in private and public spaces.

Narcissus Quagliata, born 1942 in Rome, Italy, lives in Mexico and works in USA, Europe and Asia.

beckglas@bellsouth.net

Fish Lures
cast glass, 2007

"My work in glass is a synthesis of human and mechanical form, with an emphasis on formal aspects. I am interested in playing volumes of mass against details. By extracting and exaggerating the things I find interesting in a given subject, I can reinterpret the imagery to have several meanings. Ultimately, the work should challenge the eye and the mind."

Rick Beck, born 1960 in Nebraska, lives and works in rural North Carolina.

Pull ... Earl
lampworked Pyrex glass, 2006

"I am interested in the ambiguous nature of glass and the sense of space and volume one can create. Often informed by our natural world, these works offer a new approach to working with and perhaps solving those mysteries."

Inspired by a demolition he witnessed near his studio in an industrial neighborhood in Cleveland, Kee Young translated a giant mass of tangled rebar into random matrices made from slender canes of clear Pyrex. These works are named the Matrix series and create a visual pattern of an intricately layered glass web to form unique and technically complex structures. They are entirely linear with no solid mass; geometric form within geometric form. Each presents a delicate balance of slender twigs of clear glass.

Brent Kee Young, born 1946 in Los Angeles, CA, lives and works in Cleveland, OH.

I'll Watch the Road and You Dream (group of 5 panels)
kilnformed, cameo-engraved glass, 2007
By the Guidance of the Crow (group of 3 panels)
kilnformed, cameo-engraved glass, 2007

"In a day and age when travel has become a commodity, our exposure to different cultures and places is changing our identities, morals, beliefs and art. My work is both a record and reaction to our global communities and life as I experience it, keeping in mind that everything is only as I perceive it to be and nothing is as it appears. Questioning the way that I see and understand myself through my surroundings, I capture what I have discovered to tell silent stories of contemporary life."

April Surgent, born 1982 in Missoula, MT, lives and works in Seattle, WA.

www.karenlamonte.com

Pianist's Dress
cast glass, 2005

"I feel the most important visual experience is making out an obscure image, like seeing trees through the fog, and as your pupils dilate you actually make out what the form is. It is active viewing, a visual epiphany. This is why I like to work with veiled, semi-obscured layers and semi-transparency in the prints, the mirrors, and the cast dresses. The visual experience hopefully parallels an intellectual one."

Karen LaMonte, born 1967 in Manhattan, NY, lives and works in Prague, Czech Republic.

On loan from the Gordon Sondland & Katherine Durant art collection.

Chandelier
blown and mirrored glass, 2007

Born into a family that had owned glass and antiques galleries for generations, it was only natural for Micheluzzi to be interested in glass. He was also fortunate to have the tutelage of two scions of the best-known art glass families of Venice, Laura de Santillana and the great Archimede Seguso. The chandelier at the Murano is the largest piece that he has ever created. It can be said that he uses traditional techniques to achieve a uniquely modern aesthetic.

Massimo Micheluzzi, born 1957 in Venice, Italy, lives and works in Venice, Italy.

Spingarpa
carved & blown glass, 2007

"Unlike various other art forms, with glasswork it is essential for the participant to use his sense of touch. I encourage my audience to have a real encounter with each piece: I want them to touch it, to caress it, and to understand the shapes and movements. Simply, I want the enthusiast to experience what I feel for my art, the passion and the love."

Salvadore is inspired by Africa and, using a lively visual language, he reinterprets and reinvigorates traditional African symbols. He uses mostly earth tones in his work, punctuated by splashes of brilliant color that bring to mind the bright hues of African textiles. Areas of intense carving create rhythm while the sensuous, organic forms of his work appear at times to breathe.

Davide Salvadore, born 1953 on Murano, Italy, lives and works on Murano, Italy.

On loan from the Gordon Sondland & Katherine Durant art collection.

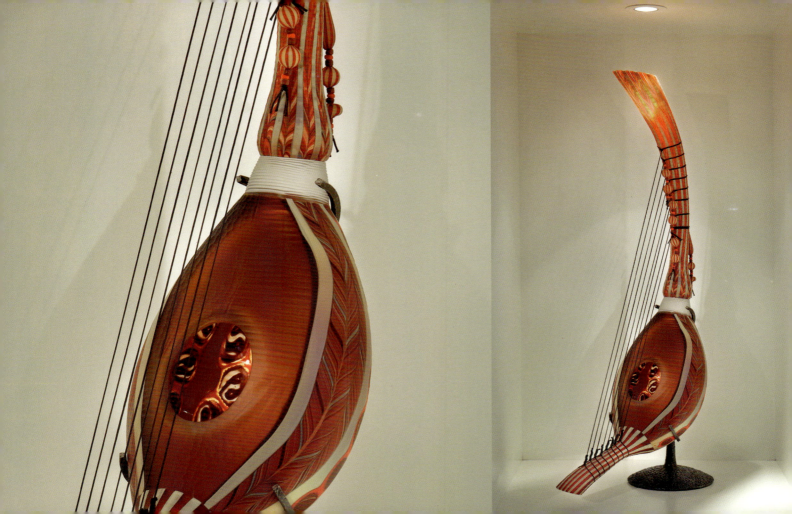

Creation
lampworked & blown glass, 2007

Bubacco's fascination with anatomy, equine and human, allows him to push beyond the perceived limits of lampworking. He works with Murano soda glass canes (also called "soft glass") rather than the less-fragile Pyrex glass and his large, freestanding sculptures are worked hot and annealed during the process. His knowledge of technique and glass color compatibility allow him to create unique works; figures that are entirely hand-formed and incorporated into blown vases.

Lucio Bubacco, born 1957 on Murano, Italy, lives and works on Murano, Italy.

Series, Nested
blown glass, 1984

"I had called my friend Italo Scanga, because they were doing this catalog of my work and I said, "Italo, I've got to have a name for this new series, these brightly spotted pieces. I think I'm going to call them the Spotted series." He said, "No, that's a terrible name." And I said, "How do you say spotted in Italian?" He's from Italy and he said, "I can't remember. Let me go look it up and I'll call you back." He called back and said, "Macchia. Macchia, that's a great name." So I call it the "Macchia" series, which is 'spotted' in Italian. I still do some of the kind of transparent pieces, a holdover from the sea form series. These Macchia pieces remind me of the sea, the deep sea, too."

Hotel Murano is fortunate to own The Macchia Series piece that is displayed in the lobby and the eight original color crayon drawings that are displayed on the mezzanine floor. They were bought when the original hotel was built in 1984.

Dale Chihuly, born 1941 in Tacoma, WA, lives and works in Seattle, WA.

Grand Corridor | Alison Kinnaird   www.alisonkinnaird.com

Interface
wheel engraved, sand blasted, cast glass, 2007

"The purity of the medium adds a spiritual dimension – its transparency and mirror surfaces give different insights on the human condition. In more than one way one can 'see through' the images engraved on its surfaces. Often I use the glass in its character of a window or a doorway, sometimes to suggest isolation or entrapment, sometimes with the figures poised between two worlds. Sometimes they confront an opposite or a mirror image. Glass is a surreal material – it is there and yet not there."

Alison Kinnaird, born 1949 in Edinburgh, Scotland, lives and works in Midlothian, Scotland.

Moment When Darkness
fused glass with murrine, 2007

"My work focuses on notions of perspective, and how our emotions and thoughts color and form our perspective on things. By working with pattern and layering, I wish to expose rhythmic and intricate patterns that relate to the inner workings and mysteries existing beneath the surface of our reality. It is the aspects of motion and change that I aim to convey, by relying on the moiré effect created by the specific processes that I employ to make my work."

Janice Vitovsky, born 1977 in Adelaide, Australia, lives and works in Piccadilly, Australia.

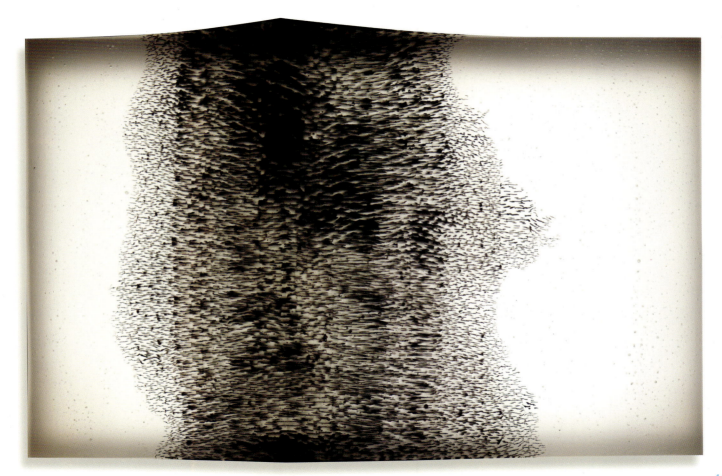

Musicale
kilnformed glass, 2004

"Drawing is the most delicate link to memory; it is intuition, it is breath, a pathway between ourselves and our world."

A draftsman without bounds, creator of drawings in media ranging from paper to video to kiln-glass, Donzelli is a relentless thinker who makes poetry of the infinite possibilities of human action and perception.

Maurizio Donzelli, born 1958 in Brescia, Italy, lives and works in Brescia, Italy.

www.damogkarlslundglas.dk

Specimen Block
blown and cast glass, 2007

"I'm a qualified toolmaker. I make the glass, I do the photographing, I build the furnaces and all the studio equipment – and I grow the garden, do the plumbing, restore the windows, do some of the cooking and tend the kids. It's all the same – it's about understanding what's in front of you. In glass I skip the rules and do it exactly like I want to." (From an interview by Brett Littman for Heller Gallery.)

Steffen Dam, born 1961 in Middlefart, Denmark, lives and works near Ebeltoft, Denmark.

Balancing Act IV
kilnformed glass, 2006

"I am continually amazed by the variety of ways we human beings present ourselves to the world. Armed with a camera (or not), I find myself standing quietly aside so as to observe the ebb and flow of the communities I temporarily inhabit. My observational photographs illustrate how things appeared at the very moment the shutter clicked. They are precisely what the camera saw. These assorted snippets of photographed time and space are now isolated elements, alienated from accurate and cohesive narrative. As, are we.

The very act of rendering is, of course, subjective. Fighting the narrative urge, I offer these individuals as I have seen each one during the act of image-making. Out of context. Alone together. As is."

Catharine Newell, born 1947 in Pasadena, CA, lives and works in Portland, OR.

a.gambale@libero.it

Tipo Veneziano
fused glass, 2001

Tipo Veneziano is one of a series of glass portraits of different Italian types. Paola Tognon writes, "If you study the glass portraits carefully, one could say that they are a multifaceted self portrait. Each one has a resemblance to Alberto. These works represent the capacity of an artist able to play with the irony of his own multiplication through the medium of glass."

Alberto Gambale, born 1963 in Ferrara, Italy, lives and works in Ferrara, Italy.

Bee Deva
painted glass, 2007

"My emotions are stirred by such things as naïve symbolic drawings, flat perspectives, and dream-like qualities found in primitive painting and in folk arts. Magic is in the wildly imaginative mythic figures, jewel-toned landscapes and anthropomorphized animals of Persian miniatures and Indian painting. This experience feeds my imagination and nurtures my soul. I believe that I had this same kind of experience hearing fairy tales as a child. In my work I am aspiring to create this experience for the viewer, to be emotionally transported by a story, and to resonate with its meaning."

Cappy Thompson, born 1952 in Alexandria, VA, lives and works in Seattle, WA.

Landscape in White
flame-worked, etched glass, 2009

"Though my glass art is formally directed at fully realizing a synergy of two- and three-dimensional forms and shapes within a fully developed formal color context, the realization of the art has been in representing human figures in flame-worked glass and presenting them in a context or juxtaposition which creates a narrative communication with the viewer. The figures are usually representational, but they are subservient to the more pervasive demands of the narrative in which they are placed. Because the narrative is intended to be interactive with the viewer, the figures are made and positioned in a suggestive, rather than explicit, narrative context relative to each other. Manifold interpretations of the interactions of the figures are intended and encouraged by the context in which they are placed and presented. The interaction with the viewer is intended to be both visceral and intellectual."

Pat Owens, born 1942 in Kansas, lives and works in N. Wales, PA.

Still Life I
painted, etched glass montage, 2000

"My inspiration is almost always the same. It is what I know well: friends, relationships, relationships between man and women. My personal ones and the general ones, those of the present, and the past."

Dana Zameçnikova, born 1945 in Prague, Czech Republic, lives and works in Prague, Czech Republic.

Biot Triptych
etched, screen printed glass montage

"My work combines photography and glass, using montage, layering and lighting to produce the final pieces. The images are screen printed onto the glass which is then fired, etched and hand painted. Many works are based on photographs documenting significant change in East London over the past several years."

Deborah Sandersley, born 1968 in London, England, lives and works in London, England.

The Viking Boats
kilnformed, slumped, fused, coldworked glass, 2007

"I find inspiration in mythology, fantasy and dreams, and when I make bigger things like the Viking Boats I need the stories to hold it all together."

Three Viking boats were commissioned by the hotel to hang in the atrium above the ballroom corridor. The largest depicts the myths of the Viking gods; the medium-sized boat features the goddesses whose lives were so intertwined with the gods; the smallest depicts the destruction of the Nordic gods and the birth of Christianity.

Vibeke Skov, born 1954 in Odense, Denmark, lives and works in Søhuset, Denmark.

Named "Boat of the Gods," the largest boat depicts the bloodthirsty myths of the great Nordic gods. Approximately 60 kiln-formed, fused, and cold-worked panels invite you into a world of evil serpents, battling warriors, and raging storms that underlie these heroic ancient stories.

The medium boat is named "Boat of the Goddesses." Its 50 or so panels share some of the lesser-known myths about the magical Nordic goddesses, their lives intertwined with the gods, and their stories of great importance in the old Norse legends.

"The Creation Boat" is the smallest boat. The stories it tells on its 40+ panels depict the birth of the Nordic pantheon, and its destruction. The Norse gods knew an Armageddon, or 'Ragnerok,' would destroy them, and so it did. What would rise from the bloody chaos was a new world order: Christianity.

Oakland Deck
mixed media

Thermon is known as an innovator. Throughout his career he has pushed the boundaries of his medium – challenging us to look at glass in new and interesting ways. His work displays a refreshing curiosity and child-like innocence, while at the same time demonstrating wit, wisdom and self-confidence. The charm of his work is that it keeps us guessing.

Therman Statom, born 1953 in Winterhaven, FL, lives and works Omaha, NE.

Laudes Regiae
multi media, blown glass, video, music installation, 2006

This installation was first shown in the exhibition space of the Convent of Saints Cosma and Damian on the island of Guidecca in Venice in 2007. It consists of 17 frosted blown glass helmets, of imagery of the Wolf of Passau (the image emblazoned on the swords produced in the Middle Ages in the village of Passau) and of the audio track of the so-called Laudes Regiae, the chorus of the Crowning Mass taken from the Bramburg Manuscript.

"The diversity of languages and means which I employ in order to realize my ideas prevents me from being identifiable; it can be said that my works, though extremely heterogeneous, have a common search to emotionally involve the spectator in order to stimulate reflections which range from spiritual questions to extremely current socio-political themes."

Andrea Morucchio, born 1967 in Venice, Italy, lives and works in Venice, Italy.

Remember me in January
Fused, kilnformed glass 2007

"When I see an old oak, I think about what an incredible life it has had, always growing, always blooming and giving shelter to thousands of creatures, surviving things that would kill me in a short time ... What I do with my work is a respectful translation in glass of a little part of our wonderful world where I have been in the company of trees."

Miriam's work pays tribute to the gentle forests and rivers south of Milan where she lives. All of her life, forests have had a deep and symbolic meaning for her.

Miriam di Fiore, born 1959 in Argentina, lives and works in Mornica Losana, Italy.

ARGENTINEAN MIRIAM DI FIORE'S WORK PAYS TRIBUTE TO THE GENTLE
FORESTS AND RIVERS SOUTH OF MILAN WHERE SHE NOW LIVES. ALL OF
HER LIFE, FORESTS HAVE HAD A DEEP AND SYMBOLIC MEANING FOR HER.

The Bathers
etched, blown glass 2007

"It always intrigues me when the forms reveal a negative space that is as vital and potent as the actual objects."

In Martin's abstract scenes the vibrant, repetitive structures inherent in nature become exposed. Their diverse forms repeat, flowing to create a passage, a line, a twist, and an eddy that continually impact, and are themselves continually impacted by, their surroundings. The original charcoal figure studies by Martin in each meeting room on the mezzanine floor demonstrate that he is as proficient in two-dimensional work as he is in three.

Martin Blank, born in 1962 in Boston, MA, lives and works in Seattle, WA.

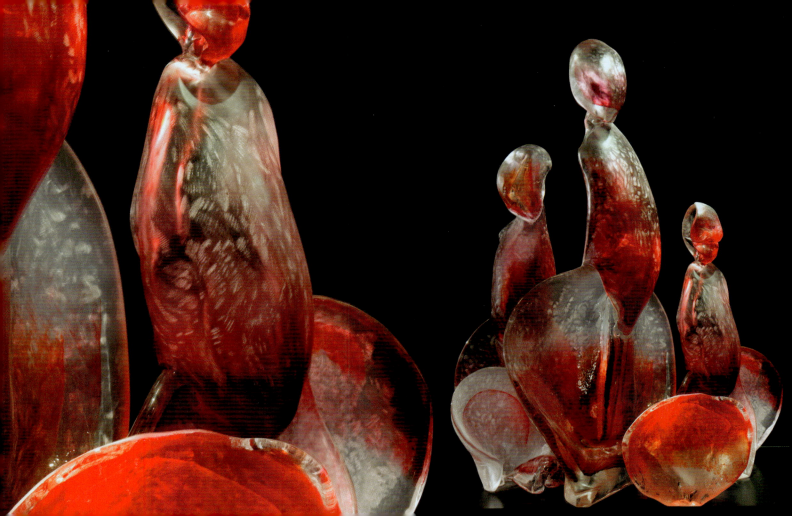

Nests
blown glass 2007

"My work is about using the Venetian techniques in a Scandinavian way. It is also about seeing the technique as a tool to clarify and refine my personal expression. I have searched for simple details in glass which, when used in the right context, add a refinement to the end result. I have explored methods to break away from the traditional patterns to discover a new and more organic expression and style."

Tobias Møhl, born in 1970 in Aalborg, Denmark, lives and works in Ebeltoft, Denmark.

Homage to the Implant
blown glass, 2007

"Femininity, philosophy, media, and the human form all play key roles in order to gain a greater understanding of my subject."

Using glass as an "instigator" Townsend creates personal commentaries that oftentimes speak to the ideals of perfection we all strive for, whether we're aware of it, or not. In *Homage to the Implant*, her shiny-and-new blown glass lineup of "the perfect pair" alludes to society's consumerism; it's prêt-à-porter perfection.

"The perfect face, the perfect breasts, the perfect home! All women strive for perfection – in a search for perfection are we losing a grasp of reality?"
- Germaine Greer, *The Whole Woman*, 2002

Jessica Townsend, born in 1983 in England, lives and works in Essex, England.

Akhenaton
pate de verre, 2002

"I am hoping to initiate an interactive experience, to encourage each person to delve into their imagination and write their own story."

Randal is an American artist but his inspiration is from the ancient worlds of Egypt, Greece, and Rome. He follows the centuries-old Platonic principle that speaks to beauty as an inherent part of an object, not something bestowed on it by the viewer: for Plato, and Randal, beauty can never be separated from the object it possesses.

Seth Randal, born in 1958, New York, lives and works in Los Angeles, California.

On loan from the Gordon Sondland & Katherine Durant art collection.

76

Purse
cast glass, 2006

"(Glass) insists we look into it, that we do not stop at the surface of what is shown."

Influenced by the cultures of Poland, Denmark and now the USA, Walentynowicz is more sensitive than most to cultural differences. His ironically titled *Guns Save Lives* series expresses his views of the violence he sees as an integral part of American society that's always present if you look deep enough.

Janusz Walentynowicz, born in 1956 in Poland, lives and works in Illinois, USA, and in Denmark.

Balance 52
kilnformed, blown, coldworked glass, 2006

"I am challenged by that act of balancing and this is what my work addresses. Through the use of shape, color, stripes, line, texture, and the incomparable reflection of light that only glass can provide, I create situations that question this balance."

Klein seeks to explore and have fun with the fragile state of balance. In everyday life, he feels, there are moments that require compromise, resolution, and action to create a sense of harmony.

Steve Klein, born in 1946 in Los Angeles, lives and works in California.

Blue Fin
cast glass, 2001

"For the past ten years my work has been an exploration of space and form using glass as a substrate activated by light. The fundamental material qualities of glass, transparency, translucency and reflection, are agents within the work that create the dialogue between voids and solids. The language of architectural form and industrial shapes strongly influences my practice as I am most interested in the tension and ambiguity between what is man-made and what is organic. I see very close parallels between bodies and buildings and, through the interplay of positive and negative space, they allude to personal and psychological space."

Richard Whiteley, born in 1963 in England, lives and works in Queanbeyan, Australia.

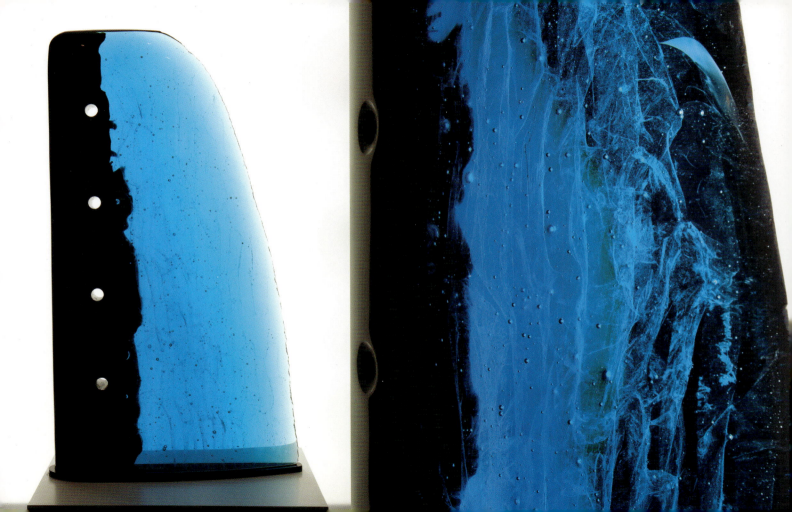

Shifting Seasons
kilnformed, hot-formed & coldworked glass, 2006

"The major inspirations behind my current work are the unique beauty of the natural environment and our ability to gather natural fibers from it to create hand-woven, nurturing forms. In producing this body of work, it was important for me to combine this fascination with my personal experience as a young mother and artist and to produce tactile glass objects that echoed life and celebrated growth within this rich landscape."

Cobi Cockburn, born in 1979 in Sydney, Australia, lives and works in Shoalhaven Heads, NSW, Australia.

Trio
blown glass, 2006

"I started blowing glass and discovered that I liked tall and thin forms, and my pieces have gradually gotten that way. When I make drawings, that's the way they come out: tall and thin. It can take me several years before I am able to make what I have drawn. My eye has evolved too. Looking at slides of my earlier work, I remember at the time I thought my vessels were perfect. Now I look at this work and I see that I am much better today at what I do."

Dante Marioni, born in 1964 in Mill Valley, CA, lives and works in Seattle, WA.

On loan from the Gordon Sondland & Katherine Durant art collection.

86

Happily Ever After
fused, sewn glass, 2006

"My life and art are the result of homemaking gone awry. I have the luxury of exploring the complexities of domestic life from the safe distance of my studio."

Taylor Glasgow's mother told her she should always act like a lady, and, as men appreciated it, she must learn to cook and sew. Today Taylor Glasgow says her misguided domestic talents grew into concepts of sewing an unyielding medium, baking inedible creations, and stitching glass clothing no one can wear. For many years she thought her art was about herself but she has recently come to realize that it is mostly about her mother, about the sewing and cooking skills and the domesticated feminine ideals she passed on. Taylor Glasgow's work embraces these ideals but in a contrary material, which offers conflicting messages of comfort and expectation.

Susan Taylor Glasgow, born in 1962 in Duluth, MN, lives and works in Columbia, MI.

Bowled Over
blown glass, 2006

"Not knowing where my work will lead enriches the mystery of the creative process and keeps me honest!"

Perkins imbues her bowling balls and pins with unexpected emotion and a light-hearted surrealism. The forms may appear simple, but the technique of blowing them has taken eight years of experimentation. She follows hunches and is evolving a personal iconography and style that is increasingly recognized.

Flo Perkins, born 1951, California, lives and works in Santa Fe, NM.

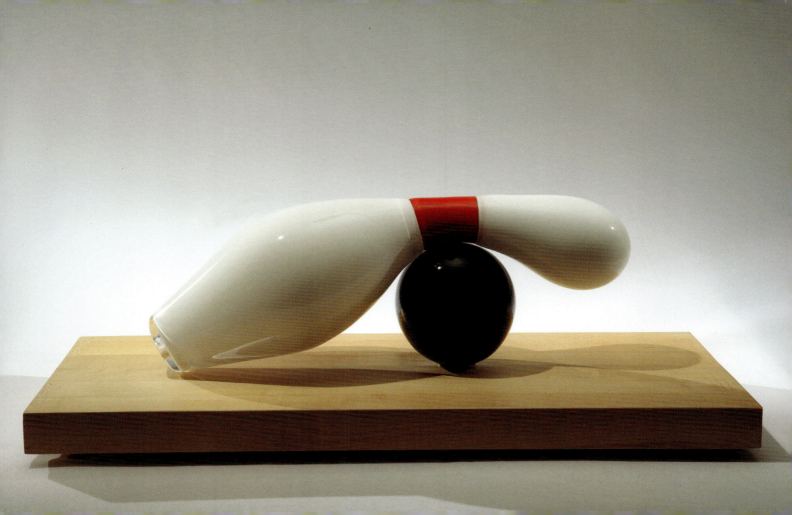

Ventura
filet de verre, 2007

"The time to physically wander, to let our minds wander, to daydream, has become much undervalued. Our minds often do their best thinking without our conscious interference."

The critic Arthur C. Danto says of Zynsky's work, "In an age in which the relevance of beauty to art is widely questioned, Zynsky's work is uncompromisingly beautiful. The intensity of adjoined color, the tactile vitality of fluted walls, the swirling energies of shape and pattern are transformed into a luminous whole through the interaction between glass and light."

Toots Zynsky, born 1952, Boston, MA, lives and works in Providence, RI.

Journey X
cast glass, 2007

"A violent transformation does take place in the cooling oven. When the sculpture is pried out and removed from the cooler, the tale the sculpture tells is captured for eternity in the glass, and only internal fires can restore it to its original form."

The cast ship form and its symbolism have been recurring themes in Vallien's work. He says, "The ship is a perfect expression of loneliness. It is evocative of femininity, of adventure, of catastrophe, a thin protective shell that demands absolute respect of all aboard. It is a society in isolation, a self-contained world afloat on the sea."

Bertil Vallien, born 1938, Stockholm, Sweden, lives and works in Småland region of Sweden.

Oyster Catcher Rattle
blown, sand carved glass, 2006

"The Bird Rattles have sculpted figures with stylized bodies and cast faces. These pieces refer to the animal spirits sharing their power and knowledge with human beings."

Singletary has been described as an "urban Indian" who has chosen to reconnect with his Tlingit heritage and culture through the medium of glass. By infusing traditional design with fresh energy, his work pays homage to his forefathers, who felt that the past, present and future are intertwined.

Preston Singletary, born 1963, San Francisco, CA, lives and works in Seattle, WA.

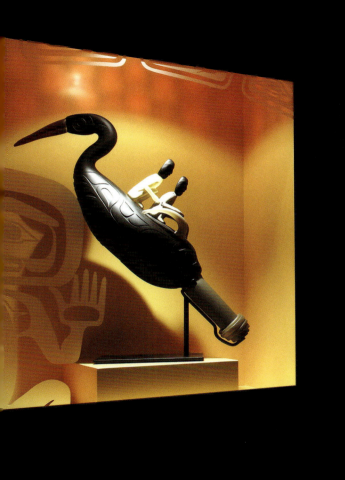

Face to Face
cast glass, 2007

"I like to express many visible things – like memory, dream, and various change of emotion – with my figurative objects. I hope that everyone who sees my work feels their own memory, and stops to speak with it."

Masayo Odahashi, born 1978, Mie, Japan, lives and works in Osaka, Japan.

Sleep of Reason
cast glass, 2004

"Like photographs, they represent moments in time, but are captured in glass leaving an impression behind. The body was once there but now only the 'Memory' remains. This body of work is concerned with perceptions of memory, of masculinity and of identity. It takes the form of casts from life. Some of the pieces explore this idea further; the image of the body is not actually there and what is now the object is the space around the body."

Bruno Romanelli, born 1968, England, lives and works in London, England.

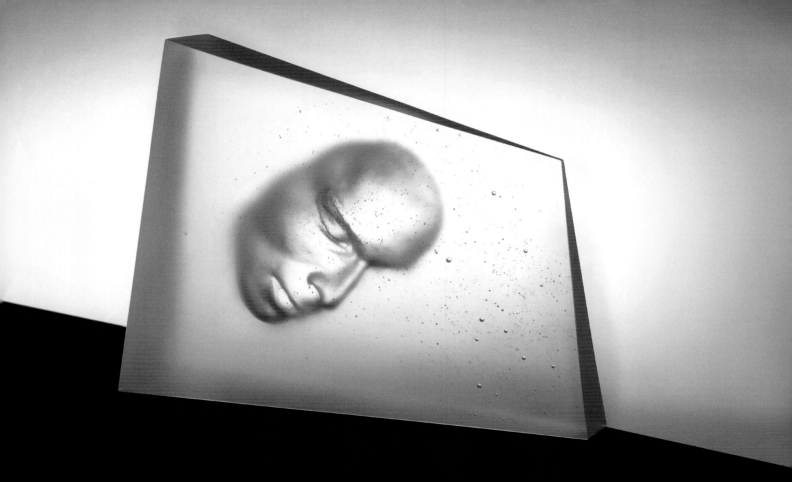

Essential Self
slumped glass, 2007

"My work is metaphorical and allusive, but in loose felt ways, rather than by the use of conscious specific references. I'm usually seeking qualities of antiquity and mystery, something unmoored from time and place. I strive for work that projects a feeling of obscure provenance and yet evokes feelings of deep recognition and connection."

While Powning's award-winning work is shown internationally, it is imbued with qualities distilled from a life lived close to the silence, space and seasonal rhythms of his home, the fields, forests and shorelines of Canada's East Coast.

Peter Powning, born 1949 in Providence, RI, lives and works in New Brunswick, Canada.

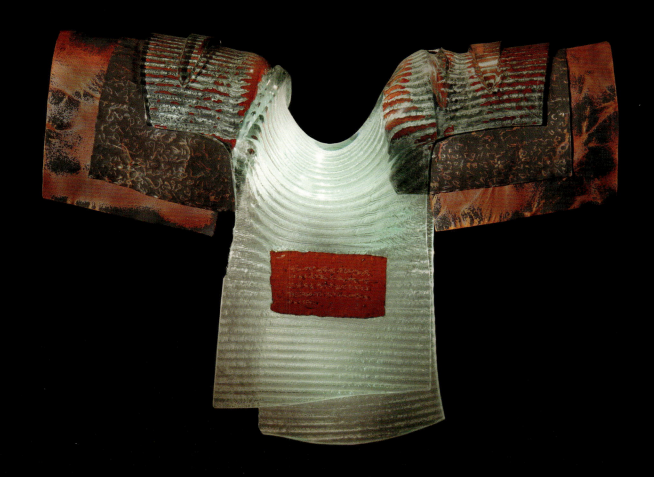

Fish Hanger #49
blown, hot sculpted glass, 2005

"I am a fish who is always looking for something. I am a fish who cannot stop swimming until my body stops moving. Maybe I'll swim forever, like the universe."

Yamano has long identified with fish swimming the oceans, as he so often traverses the vast waters between continents in his own life. His Nagare (a Japanese word meaning current) pieces are designed to be slightly askew, creating a sense of movement, or flow, in the work. They are an extension of his popular From East to West series, through which he explores the influence of both Eastern and Western cultures in his life.

Hiroshi Yamano, born 1956 in Fukuoka, Japan, lives and works in Fukuoka, Japan.

Iceberg
cast glass, 2007

"I can only say that, for me, the overwhelming emotion was my sense of insignificance in the face of the savage energy of the oceans and of the delight at the sight of yet another majestic sunrise over a flawless snow-covered landscape. How can I express my gratitude for this inexhaustible source of inspiration other than by trying to depict the awesome power and majesty of nature in my sculpture? Not aiming to imitate or equal it, but simply to express my sense of wonder as a human being and an artist."

"We see the natural world as something separate from ourselves. We exploit its gifts without restraint for economic gain, and by doing so turn it from an age-old friend into a hostile force."

Peter Bremers, born 1957 in Maastricht, Netherlands, lives and works in southern Netherlands.

Idolito
blown glass, 2004

"Glassblowing is the closest thing to alchemy that I know of."

For over twenty years Morris has created hauntingly beautiful glass sculptures that speak of myth, ancestry and ancient civilizations. They appear to be of ancient stone or of carved wood, not the modern glass that they actually are. The South American author, Isabel Allende, puts it another way, "The first time I saw William Morris's Idols I felt an electric thrill ... it was like finding myself before the intangible beings I had been looking for all my life, that I had glimpsed in my dreams and evoked in my writing."

William Morris, born 1957 in Carmel, CA, lives and works north of Seattle, WA.

Ripple
blown glass, 2003

"My pieces are typically narrative, working mainly with figurative elements and symbolic objects. Much of my current work is influenced by mans' relationship with nature, as well as his impact upon nature. I find faces and hands to be very beautiful and expressionistic, a source of silent communication, and I use gestures and titles to help convey an overall story. My pieces are usually about communication with self, or between others."

Ross Richmond, born 1970, lives and works in Seattle, WA.

Tessa Papas | Art Consultant + Curator

Over the past forty years Tessa Papas has accumulated a large and cosmopolitan reservoir of knowledge in many aspects of the art and design worlds. An artist in her own right, she has had a number of one woman exhibitions in Greece, Switzerland and USA. She married the prominent political cartoonist, Bill Papas, and up until his death in 2000 handled his career as a well known watercolorist, illustrator and cartoonist. She has owned galleries in Greece and in USA and worked closely with artists of many different nationalities. She has written several books. She has lived in many different countries and she speaks good French and Greek. She has access to and has worked with an extremely talented group of interior & graphic designers, project managers, printers, installers, glaziers, cabinet makers etc. This multifaceted life experience, her innate "eye" for art and design and her ability to attain excellent rapport with everyone she works with has made her uniquely qualified to put together meaningful collections of art for any business or individual.

"With everyone from Dale Chihuly to Karen LaMonte, ... as well as a roster of international glass virtuosos, the hotel rivals an art expo in the breadth of work on display." - Glass Quarterly | "As a kind of tribute to the Washington state city famous for glass, Tacoma's Hotel Murano literally shimmers." - Globe & Mail Toronto | "On every guest room floor, the visitor is greeted with a highlighted artist, his or her story and a final masterpiece." - Hotel Designs | "...spectacular art is only part of the appeal at the sophisticated, modern 320-room hotel..." - Alaska Airlines Magazine | "...destined to become a piece of public art." - Tacoma News | "An inspired hotel in Washington State celebrates glassmaking as an art form." - Conde Nast Traveller (UK) | "This varied collection by contemporary artists makes the hotel a must-stay..." - Corning Museum of Glass | "Hotel Murano – Judges' Award for the best use of art" - Hospitality Design Magazine | "With a collection of glass that ranges stylistically from representational to highly conceptual and in scale from intimate to truly grand, few visitors to the Hotel Murano will be able to say that this is something they've never seen anywhere before." - City Arts Magazine

Additional pieces on loan from the Gordon Sondland & Katherine Durant art collection:

Gallery Room:
Andy Warhol
Campbell's Soup Can I - Vegetable (F&S 48), 1968
serigraph, ed 233/250

Lobby:
Chuck Close
James , 2005
color screenprint, 6/80

Bite Restaurant:
Eva and Franco Mattes
Portrait series, 2006
color digital prints